Sashing separates the blocks in a quilt design, and borders frame the quilt. Both should be chosen carefully.

The sashing strips may be placed horizontally and vertically, or they may be placed diagonally. Once the blocks are completed, you may want to experiment with various widths of sashing. Sashing may be made from contrasting or background fabric and may be solid or pieced.

Make the final decision on a border design after the blocks and sashing are stitched together. A simple design that works well is a narrow, dark border next to the blocks, with a wide, lighter border around the outside. This sets off the piecing and unifies the quilt top.

How to Make Sashing Strips with Connecting Squares

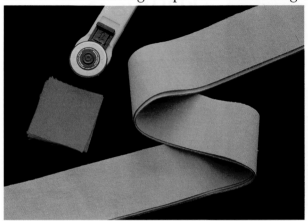

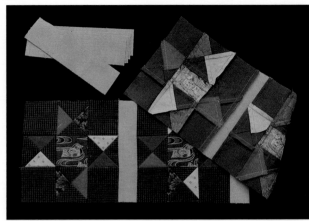

1) Cut strips to desired width of sashing plus ½" (1.3 cm) for seam allowances. Cut squares for corners from contrasting fabric the width of sashing.

2) Measure all sides of several blocks to determine shortest measurement; cut sashing strips this length. Stitch strips between blocks, right sides together, to form rows; ease in fullness. Do not stitch strips to ends of rows. Press seam allowances toward strips.

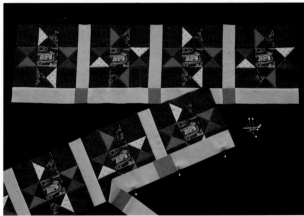

3) Stitch the remaining sashing strips alternately to sashing squares, to equal length of block and sashing row. Press seam allowances toward sashing strips.

4) Place sashing unit along bottom of first row of blocks, right sides together, matching seams. Pin along length, easing in any fullness; stitch. Repeat for remaining rows, except for bottom row.

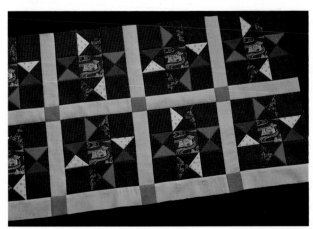

5) Pin bottom of one long sashing strip to top of next row, matching seams, as in step 4; stitch. Press seam allowances toward sashing strip. Continue until all rows are attached.

Alternate design. Make connecting checkerboard squares. Choose a width for sashing and finished squares that can be easily divided by 3.

How to Make a Border with Interrupted Corners

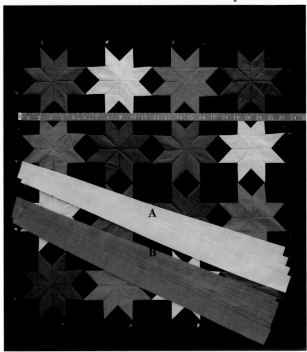

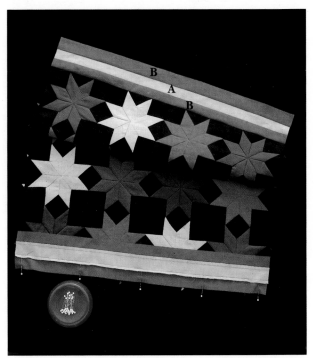

1) Measure top and bottom rows of the quilt top to determine the shorter measurement. Cut four strips of Fabric A and eight strips of Fabric B, with length equal to shorter measurement and width equal to one-third the finished width of border plus ½" (1.3 cm). Measure sides of quilt and cut strips as above.

2) Sew strips together for top and bottom of quilt top to form two B-A-B units. Pin one pieced border to top of quilt, right sides together, at center and two ends; pin along length, easing in any fullness. Stitch. Press seam allowance toward border. Repeat with remaining unit at bottom.

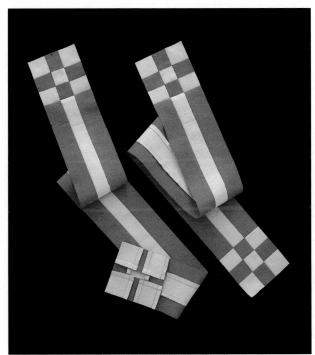

3) Sew strips together for sides to form two B-A-B units. Make four 9-patch blocks, using same width measurements as in step 1, above. Stitch one block to each end of border strips. Press seam allowances toward borders.

4) Pin and stitch the borders to sides of quilt, as in step 2, above, matching seams at corners. Press seam allowances toward border.

Frame Sashing

Frame sashing is pieced to form a unique design of parallelograms and triangles. For easy construction, the sashing pieces are stitched to each quilt block. When the framed blocks are stitched together, the sashing forms an eight-pointed star where the corners of four blocks meet, and the pieced triangles form squares in the design.

The unpieced quilt blocks, cut from a single fabric, may be embellished with quilting or appliqués. The sashing is constructed from gradations of a color. The choice of color in the sashing can create either a subtle frame around each block or a bold design.

The instructions that follow are for a bed quilt. For a twin-size, which measures about 68" × 86" (173 × 218.5 cm), three rows of two blocks are pieced. For a full/queen-size, which measures about 86" (218.5 cm) square, three rows of three blocks are pieced. The sashing is constructed around 12" (30.5 cm) quilt blocks. Each block framed with

3" (7.5 cm) sashing measures 18" (46 cm) square. Wide 16" (40.5 cm) borders complete the quilt and provide a background for decorative quilting. To eliminate the need for piecing, the border strips are cut on the lengthwise grain.

✄ Cutting Directions

Cut two 3½" (9 cm) strips of each of the eight solid-colored fabrics for sashing; these will be cut into parallelograms (page 7).

Cut the four fabrics for sashing triangles into 7¼" (18.7 cm) squares; for a twin-size quilt, cut two squares of each fabric, and for a full/queen-size quilt, cut three squares of each fabric. Cut all squares diagonally in both directions, making four triangles from each square.

For the quilt blocks, cut 12½" (31.8 cm) fabric strips; cut the strips into squares, cutting six for a twin-size quilt and nine for a full/queen-size.

YOU WILL NEED

For twin-size:

¾ yd. (0.7 m) fabric, to be used for quilt blocks.

¼ yd. (0.25 m) each of eight solid-colored fabrics for sashing parallelograms; choose eight shades of one color.

Scraps or ¼ yd. (0.25 m) each of four fabrics for sashing triangles.

3¾ yd. (3.45 m) fabric, to be used for continuous-length 16" (40.5 cm) borders.

2¾ yd. (2.55 m) fabric in 90" (229 cm) width, or 5¼ yd. (4.8 m) in 45" (115 cm) width, for backing.

¾ yd. (0.7 m) fabric for binding.

Batting, sized for twin-size quilt.

For full/queen-size:

1⅛ yd. (1.05 m) fabric, to be used for quilt blocks.

¼ yd. (0.25 m) each of eight solid-colored fabrics for sashing parallelograms; choose eight shades of one color.

Scraps or ¼ yd. (0.25 m) each of four fabrics for sashing triangles.

4¼ yd. (3.9 m) fabric, to be used for continuous-length 16" (40.5 cm) borders.

2¾ yd. (2.55 m) fabric in 108" (274.5 cm) width, or 7¾ yd. (7.1 m) in 45" (115 cm) width, for backing.

¾ yd. (0.7 m) fabric for binding.

Batting, sized for full/queen-size quilt.

How to Make a Quilt with Frame Sashing

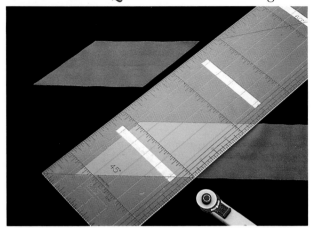

1) **Cut** a 45° angle on one end of strip for sashing. Place 4¾" (12 cm) mark of ruler along angled cut; cut strip to make parallelogram.

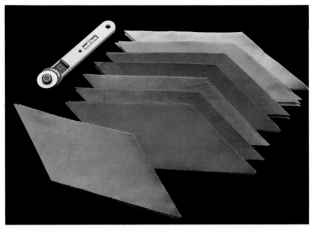

2) **Continue** cutting parallelograms from fabric strips, cutting six of each fabric for twin-size or nine of each fabric for full/queen-size.

3) **Stitch** two parallelograms of different colors to short sides of one triangle, as shown; finger-press seam allowances toward parallelograms. Trim points that extend beyond sashing.

4) **Repeat** step 3 to make four pieced sashing strips for each quilt block; randomly use each parallelogram and triangle fabric once in each set.

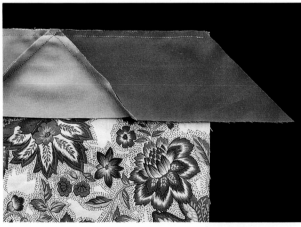

5) **Stitch** short side of one pieced sashing strip to one side of quilt block; begin and end stitching ¼" (6 mm) from edges of block, backstitching at ends. Repeat for remaining sides of block.

6) **Fold** quilt block diagonally, right sides together, matching seamlines and edges of parallelograms.

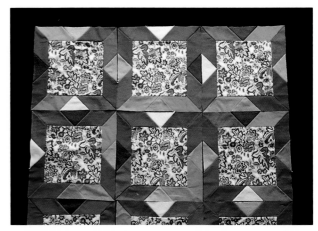

7) Stitch corner seam, backstitching at inside corner; do not catch seam allowances in stitching. Repeat for remaining corners.

8) Repeat steps 5 to 7 for remaining blocks, varying color arrangement. Arrange blocks in rows.

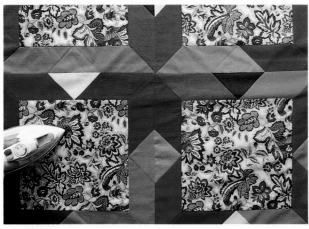

9) Stitch blocks into rows, matching points; stitch rows together, finger-pressing seam allowances at corners in opposite directions. Press the quilt top, pressing seam allowances toward blocks.

10) Cut and attach border strips, cutting strips on lengthwise grain; cut width of border strips is 16½" (41.8 cm). Mark the quilting design on border and blocks.

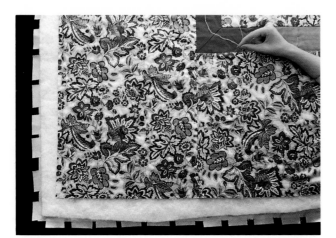

11) Cut backing and batting about 4" (10 cm) larger than quilt top. Layer and baste quilt top, batting, and backing.

12) Quilt. Cut and apply binding; cut width of binding is 2½" (6.5 cm).

Star Sashing

Sashing strips with connecting stars create a sashing design bold enough to be used with plain quilt blocks. Quick methods for cutting and piecing are used to construct the stars, making this an easy quilt project.

The instructions that follow are for a quilt made from thirty 5½" (14 cm) quilt blocks and 2¼" (6 cm) sashing. The finished quilt with a double lapped border measures about 45" × 53" (115 × 134.5 cm).

✂ Cutting Directions

Cut eight 2¾" (7 cm) strips from the fabric for the sashing strips, and cut the strips into forty-nine 6" (15 cm) rectangles. Cut two 2¾" (7 cm) strips from the fabric for the stars; cut into twenty 2¾" (7 cm) squares. Cut seven 1⅝" (4 cm) strips from the fabric for the stars; cut into 160 squares to be used for the points of the stars. For the quilt blocks, cut five 6" (15 cm) fabric strips; cut into 30 squares.

YOU WILL NEED

1 yd. (0.95 m) fabric for quilt blocks.

⅞ yd. ((0.8 m) fabric for sashing strips.

⅔ yd. (0.63 m) fabric for stars and ½" (1.3 cm) inner border.

¾ yd. (0.7 m) fabric for 3½" (9 cm) outer border.

½ yd. (0.5 m) fabric for binding.

2¾ yd. (2.55 m) fabric for backing.

Batting, about 49" × 57" (125 × 144.5 cm).

How to Make a Quilt with Star Sashing

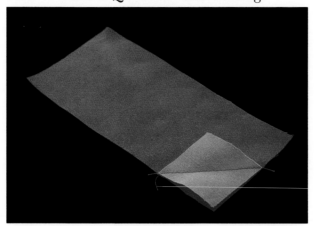

1) **Place** 1⅝" (4 cm) square in one corner of sashing strip, with right sides together and raw edges even. Stitch diagonally as shown.

2) **Press** square in half along stitched line, matching outer edges to sashing strip. Trim fabric at stitched corner, leaving ¼" (6 mm) seam allowance.

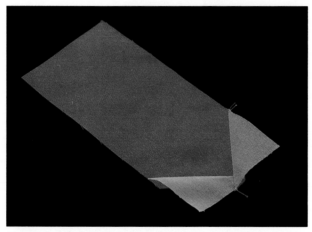

3) **Repeat** steps 1 and 2 at opposite corner. Continue piecing squares at one end of rectangles for a total of 18 pieced strips; these will be used as end strips.

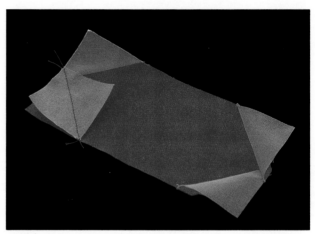

4) **Stitch** squares to all four corners of remaining sashing strips; these will be used as inner strips.

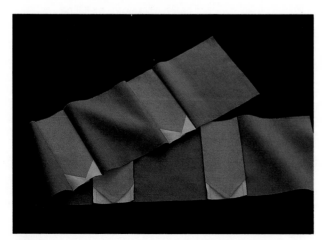

5) **Stitch** four end strips between five quilt blocks, placing plain ends at upper edge; this will be top row of quilt. Press seam allowances toward blocks.

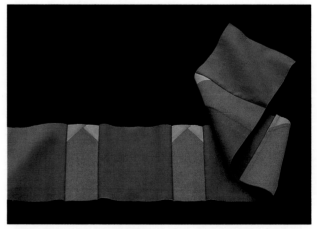

6) **Repeat** step 5 to make a second row, placing plain ends at lower edge; this will be bottom row of quilt.

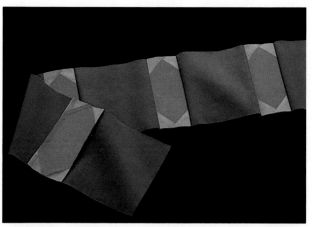

7) Stitch four inner strips between five quilt blocks to make one of the middle rows. Press seam allowances toward blocks. Repeat for three more rows.

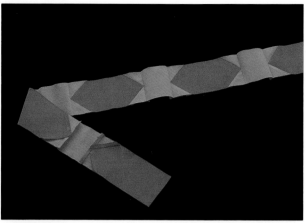

8) Stitch five sashing strips alternately to the sashing squares, using an end strip at each end. Press seam allowances toward squares. Repeat for four more rows.

9) Pin one sashing unit along bottom of top row, right sides together, matching seams; stitch. Repeat for remaining rows, except for bottom row.

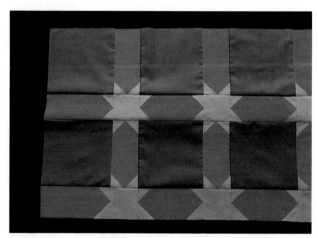

10) Pin bottom of one sashing unit to top of next row, matching seams; stitch. Continue until all rows are joined. Press seam allowances toward sashing.

11) Cut and attach border strips; cut width of border strips is 1" (2.5 cm) for inner border and 4" (10 cm) for outer border. Cut backing 4" (10 cm) larger than quilt top. Layer and baste quilt top, batting, and backing.

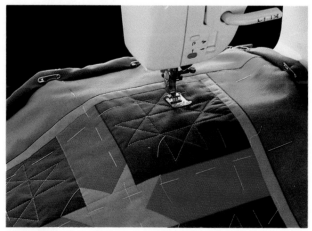

12) Quilt. Cut and apply binding; cut width of binding is 2½" (6.5 cm).

More Star Sashing Designs

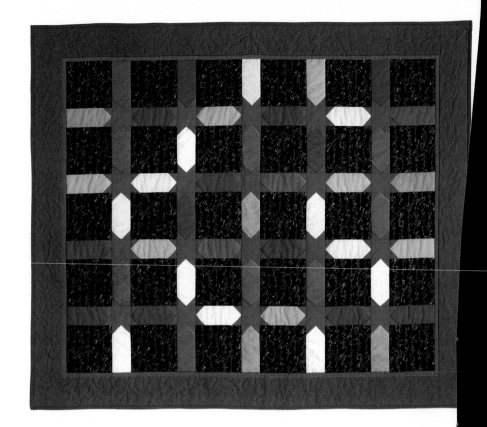

Add variety to star sashing by piecing each star in a different color or by using a gradation of colors for the sashing strips. Or for a more intricate design, use strip-pieced sashing. When using a variety of fabrics, make a sketch of the quilt for easier cutting and assembly.

Gradated colors are used for the sashing strips in the quilt at right to add subtle interest to the design.

Bright stars in a rainbow of colors are used for this child's quilt. The multicolored printed fabric in the quilt blocks adds interest to the quilt. A brightly colored stripe is used for one of the fabrics in the triple border.

Calicos and plaids create a traditional look, with template-quilted blocks complementing the style. The sashing has been strip-pieced for a more intricate design.

How to Make Strip-pieced Star Sashing

1) Cut fabric strips on crosswise grain 1¼" (3.2 cm) wide, cutting three for each row of sashing. Stitch strips together lengthwise in desired sequence, right sides together. Press.

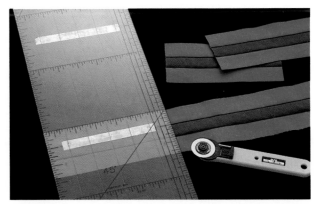

2) Cut pieced fabric into 6" (15 cm) rectangles for sashing strips. Make quilt as on pages 9 to 12.

Dark and jewel-tone fabrics create an Amish-style quilt. Strip-pieced sashing adds more interest.

Strip-pieced Sashing

Sashing with connecting squares gives a quilt an updated look when strip-pieced from gradated fabrics. Connecting squares in a bold contrasting color add another design element.

You may want to select a printed fabric for the quilt blocks and choose colors from that fabric to use for the gradation and connecting squares; the sharper the contrast, the bolder the design will be.

The instructions that follow are for a wall hanging made from nine 8" (20.5 cm) quilt blocks and 2" (5 cm) sashing. Random quilting lines complement the style of the quilt and create interest in the center of the quilt where the lines intersect. Instead of the

narrow binding that is usually used on small wall hangings, the traditional binding acts as a small border. The finished project measures about 32" (81.5 cm) square.

✂ Cutting Directions

Cut 1½" (3.8 cm) strips from each gradated color for sashing strips; cut four strips of each color from fat quarters or two strips from 45" (115 cm) yardage. Cut one 2½" (6.5 cm) fabric strip from the fabric for the connecting squares; cut the strip into sixteen 2½" (6.5 cm) squares. For the quilt blocks, cut two 8½" (21.8 cm) fabric strips; cut into nine 8½" (21.8 cm) squares.

YOU WILL NEED

⅛ yd. (0.15 m) each of eight fabrics, or one packet of hand-dyed fabrics in fat quarters, for sashing.

⅛ yd. (0.15 m) fabric for connecting squares.

¾ yd. (0.7 m) printed fabric for quilt blocks.

⅓ yd. (0.32 m) fabric for binding.

1 yd. (0.95 m) fabric for backing.

Batting, about 36" (91.5 cm) square.

How to Make a Quilt with Gradated Sashing

1) Stitch one strip of each color together lengthwise, with right sides together and in gradated sequence; repeat for remaining strips. Press seam allowances in one direction.

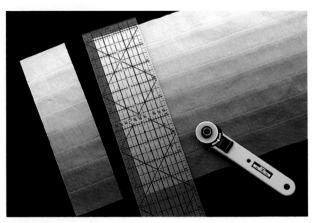

2) Cut the pieced fabric crosswise into 2½" (6.5 cm) strips, using rotary cutter.

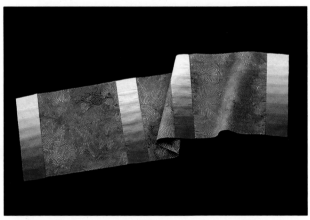

3) Stitch pieced strips between blocks, to form three rows of three blocks, with darkest color at bottom of quilt blocks; stitch pieced strips to ends of rows. Press seam allowances toward blocks.

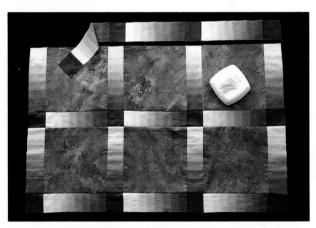

4) Complete sashing, as on page 12, steps 9 and 10; arrange strips as shown.

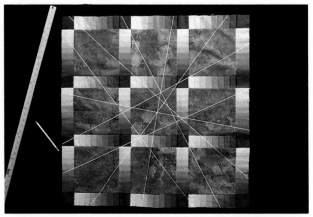

5) Mark quilting lines; draw lines randomly across quilt top, drawing about four lines from each side. Layer and baste quilt top, batting, and backing fabric. (Markings were exaggerated for clarity.)

6) Quilt along sashing, using stitch-in-the-ditch method; then quilt on marked lines. Cut and apply binding; cut width of binding is 2½" (6.5 cm).

More Strip-pieced Sashing Designs

For more colorful designs, piece fabric strips from gradated blends of two or more colors. Or cut the connecting squares from several colors. To create more motion in the quilt design, vary the arrangement of the sashing strips.

Gradated strips are arranged in the quilt at right so the dark and light colors alternately radiate from connecting squares.